CAPTAIN STARDUST
and the
Space Pirates

by David Orme
Illustrated by Tony O'Donnell

LONGMAN

SCENES

CREW OF THE SPACESHIP
STAR-CHASER

Captain Stardust, the ship's captain

Annie, the ship's scientific officer. She is an
Android (a robot built to look like a
human being).

Tom, the ship's pilot and navigator

Princess Io, captain of the pirate spaceship
Queen of the Night

Professor Arto, scientific inventor and "chief
player of dirty tricks" for
Princess Io

Hench, an unintelligent robot and servant of
Princess Io

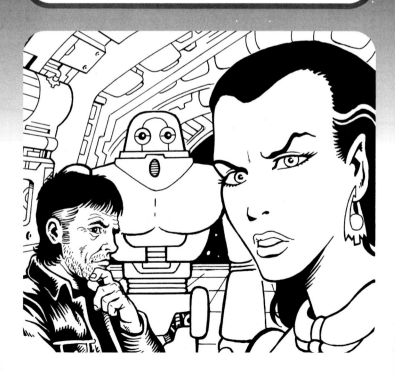

ON BOARD THE SPACESHIP
Star-Chaser

(The ship has arrived at an unexplored planet. The crew are returning from an expedition on the planet's surface.)

Stardust *(excitedly)* What a wonderful planet! I've never seen anything like those rainbow crystals before!

Annie *(in an unexcited voice)* They are certainly unusual. I have no information in my memory banks to help identify them. I would say, though, that they are made of carbon, like diamonds. They seem to grow bigger by absorbing the coal that is underneath them.

Tom Thanks for the science lesson! Don't you get excited about anything, Annie?

Annie   I am an android. I keep telling you, androids don't get excited. It's bad for their microchips.

Stardust   Well, *I'm* excited. The way those crystals change colour all the time is amazing!

Tom   Can't we take one back with us to Earth, Dusty?

Stardust   You know we can't do that, Tom. New planets mustn't be damaged or disturbed by explorers like us. Besides, the crystals might be dangerous back on Earth. Taking specimens back is strictly forbidden until scientists have checked them out. Now, we had better radio back to base to give our position. Don't say anything about the rainbow crystals, though. Those space pirates may be listening in again. I'm sure they would love to get their hands on them and make a fortune selling them.

Tom Quite right. That Princess Io and her gang have caused us enough trouble in the past. *(Sits down at the space radio.)* Hey, this radio has been left on! What idiot used it last time?

Annie You did, Tom.

Tom Oh yes, so I did. Sorry about that!

Stardust You really are an idiot, Tom! Everything we've been saying has been broadcast into space! Anyone might have been listening!

Tom Sorry, Dusty. I've turned it off now.

Stardust I just hope it's not too late!

ON BOARD THE PIRATE SHIP
QUEEN OF THE NIGHT

(Deep in space, Princess Io has been listening in to the radio.)

Io *(laughing)* It is too late, Captain Stardust! Your foolish crew have let you down again! Arto, keep listening to the space radio. As soon as the *Star-Chaser* gives its position, we'll be on our way to collect some of those rainbow crystals!

Arto They certainly sound like a wonderful scientific discovery.

Io What is more important, they are beautiful! Beautiful princesses like me need beautiful things! Besides, I've had an idea. We can make a fortune selling them.

Arto That wasn't your idea. That's what Captain Stardust said.

Io Shut up, Arto. Your job is to come up with cunning scientific inventions to further my evil plans, not to contradict me. Hench! Get me something to drink.

Hench   Yes, mistress. *(Goes out, then returns with a can of oil.)* Here you are, mistress.

Io   What's this?

Hench   Something to drink, mistress.

Io   I don't drink oil, you idiot!

Hench   I do.

Io   Arto, I thought you were going to upgrade this robot's intelligence chip!

Arto   I did. He was a moron before. Now he's just stupid.

Io   Do I have to do everything myself round here? Arto, keep listening to that radio. I'm going to get those rainbow crystals, and nothing is going to stop me!

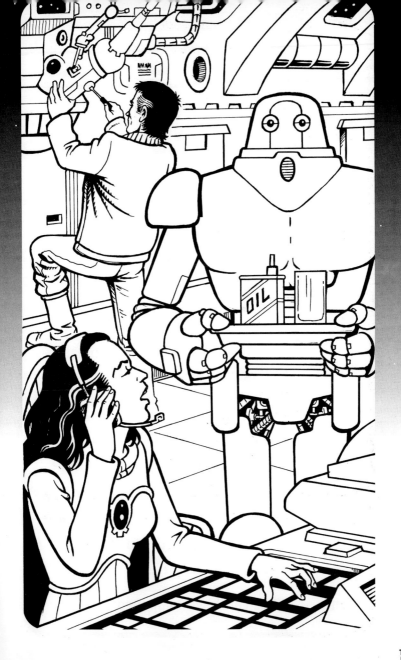

THE PLANET OF
THE RAINBOW CRYSTALS

(Captain Stardust, Annie and Tom are on another expedition on the planet's surface.)

Stardust This coal puzzles me. Coal is made from the remains of dead plants, but there are no plants on the planet.

Annie The atmosphere does not have the right gasses for plants or animals to live. You two would die if you took off your spacesuits – there's hardly any oxygen.

Tom You're right, Dusty – it certainly is a puzzle.

Annie No! Look at these fossils in these rocks! There *was* life on this planet once.

Tom What can have happened to it?

Annie   Perhaps every living thing was wiped out by a huge comet crashing into the planet.

Stardust Yes, that's possible. Some scientists think that the dinosaurs were wiped out when a comet hit the Earth millions of years ago. Hey, what are you up to, Annie?

Annie   I'm having a closer look at these rainbow crystals. Hmm, that's very interesting! Come and put your hand on one. What can you feel?

Tom   It feels just like a heartbeat!

Annie   These aren't crystals at all. They're living things!

Stardust You're right – living things, feeding off the coal. Well done, Annie!

Tom   Annie, you were almost excited there!

Annie   Sorry, Tom. I'll try not to let it happen again.

Stardust I wonder if we can communicate with them in any way?

Annie   They may not be intelligent enough for that. In any case, they don't make any sounds.

Stardust But why do they keep changing colour?

Tom   Maybe that is their way of talking to each other.

Annie   Good thinking, Tom. I will watch the colour changes carefully and see if there are any patterns.

Stardust   Hey, you two. I think we've got visitors!

Tom   I know that spaceship. That's the *Queen of the Night*. Princess Io must have overheard us, and it's all my fault!

Stardust   Let's not worry about whose fault it is. We've got a difficult situation on our hands now.

Annie   But the pirates are hoping to find precious crystals. Once we tell them that they are living things, they will go away.

Stardust   We can try it, but if I know Princess Io, that's not going to put her off. She is the most dangerous person in space! Quick, let's get back to the ship before they land. I don't want to be caught out in the open.

ON BOARD THE
QUEEN OF THE NIGHT

(*The* Queen of the Night *has landed on the rainbow planet.*)

Arto   They've just rushed back into the *Star-Chaser*.

Hench   Do you want me to go over there and smash the door down, boss?

Io   No I don't! We don't need violence to outwit them. If anything happens to Stardust and chums, we'll have the space cops after us, and those guys never give up. Come on, let's get our spacesuits on and have a look at these crystals.

Hench   Can I come? I haven't got a spacesuit!

Arto You don't need one, you clot! You're a robot! You don't need to breathe!

Hench Oh yes, I'd forgotten that.

(Meanwhile, inside the Star-Chaser*...)*

Tom   They're going outside to look at the rainbow creatures. We've got to stop them!

Stardust   I'll speak to them over their spacesuit radios. *(talking into a microphone)* Io, leave them alone. They're not crystals, they're living creatures! They live by feeding on coal.

Io   *(to Arto)* Is that right, Professor?

Arto   *(looking closely at one of the rainbow crystals)* I'm afraid so, Princess.

Io   Living creatures? That's even better! Collectors will pay a fortune for these! There's plenty of coal on Earth to feed them on now it isn't used to make energy any more. They won't cost much to feed!

Stardust   You know the penalties for taking living things away from their own planets.

Io Sorry, I've just forgotten them. So you just stay there in your spaceship while we gather up a few. I wouldn't come out if I were you. If you do, you'll have my robot Hench to deal with. So take care, Captain Stardust!

Hench Yes, take care, Captain Dustbin! I'm a very powerful robot!

Io *(in a hissing voice)* And a very stupid robot!

Hench And I'm a very stupid robot as well... Oh no, I didn't mean to say that.

Stardust *(to Annie and Tom)* Come on. We're going out. We must stop them.

Tom But what about that robot? I don't like the look of him.

Annie Nor do I – his operating system must be years out of date.

(Stardust, Tom and Annie go out onto the surface of the planet.)

Stardust Io! Don't touch those creatures!

Io So how are you going to stop me? Hench keep them away.

Hench Stand back. or I'll...

Tom What will you do?

Hench   I'll get very cross! *(He sees Annie and his voice changes.)* Who are you? You are a very beautiful creature! I want to be your friend!

Annie   Oh no! That's all I need! The crazy tin can likes me!

Tom   Hey, what's that moving over there, behind those rocks?

Stardust   They're like people, only made of rainbows! Io, look out! They're coming towards you!

Io   None of your silly tricks, Stardust!

Arto   They are behind you, and they don't look friendly! These small rainbow creatures must be their babies!

Tom   Now we're in big trouble!

Hench   *(to Annie)* Don't worry, I'll protect you! I'm a very powerful robot!

Annie   And a very stupid robot.

Hench   Yes, well, you can't have everything.

Tom   They're firing some kind of rainbow threads at us!

Stardust Quick, back into the ship.

Tom   I can't move! These threads are clinging to me!

Annie   None of us can move.

Stardust We're stuck – and they're coming closer!

A CAVE

(The crews of the Star-Chaser *and* Queen of the Night *are sitting on the floor. The door to the cave is made of steel bars to prevent them escaping. The rainbow threads have become brittle and the crews are breaking them off.)*

Io This is all your fault, Stardust!

Stardust Why me? You were the one who wanted to steal the crystals!

Io I think you left that radio on on purpose just so we would come here!

Arto Be quiet and let me think! Our air supply runs out in two hours. We must escape from here by then!

Tom What do you think the rainbow people are going to do with us?

Arto   I don't know, but if they eat the same food as their babies you had better start worrying!

Tom   But the babies eat coal!

Arto   And coal is made of carbon, and so are you, so we had better not hang around until dinner time.

Stardust Well, at least we're free of those rainbow threads.

Arto   Please be quiet! How can I come up with cunning escape plans if you keep chattering all the time!

Annie   Don't worry, professor. I think I can get us out! Look through the bars of the door. The key is on that table.

Arto   Yes, but it's too far away to reach.

Annie   I can do it. Watch! All I have to do is to take my hand off and control it with microwave signals. It can creep over the floor, climb up the table and reach the key!

Stardust Brilliant, Annie! I had forgotten you can do that!

Hench Hurrah for Annie! Give her a big hand, folks!

Annie If I had a big hand, it wouldn't get through the bars, stupid. Here it comes. I've got the key! I'll just fix my hand back on, then we're out of here!

Io Can you remember the way back to the surface?

Annie No problem. It's in my memory banks. Come on, it's this way. There's no sign of the rainbow people.

Tom Probably busy getting the oven ready for dinner.

Stardust Quiet, Tom!

Annie Don't worry, they can't hear us. They don't have ears. I am sure you are right, Tom. Those rainbow colours are their language. They talk with coloured light!

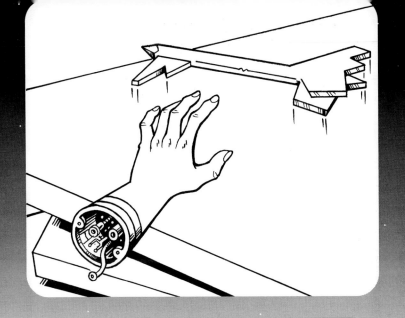

Tom   Well, unless I suddenly turn purple, we'll be all right!

Stardust What a pity we couldn't learn their language. We could have told them that we mean no harm.

Io   And you would have told them that **we** did, I suppose. Let's just get out of here. *(in a whisper)* Arto, drop back a minute. I have orders for you and I don't want the others to hear!

Arto   *(whispering)* What is it?

Io   When we get to the surface, I want you to get inside the *Star-Chaser*. I'll make Hench keep them outside. I don't want them following us back to the secret base. I want you to fix their navigating computer.

Arto   I could stop it working for a few hours to give us a chance to get away.

Io   You can do better than that. I've had enough of Stardust and company. I want you to fix the computer so it takes them straight into the nearest sun!

ON BOARD THE
Star-Chaser

(Tom is preparing for take-off.)

Tom   I really wish I knew what Arto was up to when he was in here.

Stardust   Io said that he just put a time-lock on our navigating computer to give them time to get away.

Annie   I hope that is *all* he did. Professor Arto is a clever man.

29

Stardust Can't you check the computer out, Annie?

Annie I've been trying to. This pilot's desk is so untidy, Tom! There's stuff everywhere! Why do you have to keep that picture on the desk?

Tom It's my mother. She died just after I was born. I am an orphan, you know.

Annie We androids are all orphans, Tom – we don't have parents either. I was made in a factory.

Tom I never thought of that. Hey, folks, we're in business! The computer has just come on line! Everything seems to be working normally now.

Stardust Come on, let's take off, Tom. We'll just have to take the risk that there's nothing else wrong.

Tom Righto, Captain! Firing main engines!

Stardust They will have got right away now. I would really like to know where their secret base is.

Tom Hey, Dusty, there *is* something wrong. The computer won't accept my course. It's locking me out! Do something, Annie!

Annie *(Tries to sort out the computer.)* There's nothing I can do, Tom. Professor Arto has reprogrammed it. I'd need hours to shut it down and reboot it, but it won't let me shut it down.

(A voice is heard on the radio. It is Princess Io.)

Io   *Queen of the Night* calling *Star-Chaser*! *Queen of the Night* calling *Star-Chaser*!

Stardust   What do *you* want, Io?

Io   I'm just calling to say goodbye. You're heading for the nearest sun, and there's nothing you can do about it. It's going to get very hot soon. Hope you've brought your sun cream!

Tom   It's true! We're heading straight for the sun!

Io   *(laughing)* Goodbye, Stardust! Over and out!

Stardust   It's already getting hot. In a few minutes we'll be finished!

Tom   No, it's OK! *Star-Chaser* is changing course.

Annie   Tom's right. We'll miss the sun. We're going into orbit round it!

Tom   I've got control back. We're safe!

Stardust And Io won't know. She'll think we are all cooked! Tom, swing round the sun and try and get a fix on the *Queen of the Night*.

Annie   They are much too far away by now.

Tom   They should be, but I'm getting a trace on them. Someone on the *Queen* is sending out a homing signal! We can follow them back to base!

Stardust Who's doing that? Perhaps it is that stupid robot. He wanted to be Annie's friend.

Annie   He was much too dim to be able to do that. Anyway, he wasn't very friendly when he wouldn't let us back in the ship.

Tom   Well, it's a mystery. Maybe we'll find out when we get to their secret base.

Stardust And won't they be surprised when they see us!

ON ONE OF THE MOONS OF JUPITER, NEAR THE SECRET BASE OF PRINCESS IO

(The Star-Chaser *has just landed.)*

Tom   I tracked them in, and the pirate base is just over that mountain.

Stardust It's very well hidden – no wonder the space police have never been able to find it.

Annie   Why don't we call the space police now, and let them deal with Io and her gang?

Stardust Not after that trick she tried to pull on us! No one does that to Captain Stardust! I'm going to deal with this lady myself!

Tom   We didn't actually end up in the sun though, Dusty.

Stardust No, but I'm sure that's what she wanted to happen. I expect Arto made a mistake in his calculations. Maybe he's not so brilliant after all. Get your spacesuit on, Tom! We're going to pay a visit to Princess Io! We've got a lot of walking to do, but at least the gravity is low on this moon.

Tom   Have we got to climb all the way over that mountain?

Annie   Not according to the photographs I took on the way down. There seems to be a narrow valley that splits the mountain in two. It ought to take us straight to the base.

Stardust Right, open the air-lock please, Annie! Use only your suit-to-suit radios now, we don't want Io knowing we're coming. She might just arrange a welcome party for us!

OUTSIDE THE SECRET BASE of PRINCESS IO

Tom   That was quite a walk! I thought you said it would be easy, Annie.

Annie   I said no such thing! I just said that if we went through the valley, we wouldn't have to climb over the mountain.

Tom I do seem to remember the words "straight there". What about all those twists and turns, and rocks to scramble over? It didn't seem very straight to me.

Stardust Stop moaning, Tom! We're nearly there. Personally, I enjoyed the walk. The view of Jupiter is amazing from here! It's so close!

Annie I think it would be a good idea to hide behind these rocks. There's someone over there, outside the secret base.

Stardust I wish my eyesight was good as an android's! Tell us exactly what you can see.

Annie There's someone in a spacesuit, just sitting on a rock. I think we could creep up behind without being seen.

Stardust No talking now – whoever it is might have their suit radio tuned to our channel! Watch out, it might be one of Io's tricks!

(Tom, Stardust and Annie creep up behind the figure on the rock.)

Stardust Right, whoever you are! I've got my hand on your oxygen valve! Start talking!

Annie It's Professor Arto!

Tom Arto! Chief computer meddler! Chief player of dirty tricks for Princess Io! I want a word with you!

Arto Don't be too hard on me, Tom. I did fix the computer, but I didn't do what the Princess wanted. I made sure you would miss the sun, then I switched on the beacon that would bring you here.

Stardust Don't believe him, Tom. It's just another one of Io's tricks.

Tom I don't believe him. Anyway, Arto, I don't remember saying you could call me Tom. Only my friends call me by my first name.

Arto And what is your second name?

Tom	I don't know. I am an orphan.
Arto	But I know what it is!
Tom	What do you mean?

Arto   You must believe me when I say I've finished with Io. She found out about the homing beacon. She pushed me out here to die; I've only two hours' worth of oxygen left.

Annie   How can you prove that? Why would you betray your leader?

Arto   Tom – please let me call you that – I have a good reason: there is a photograph on your desk. Who is the person in the photograph?

Tom   My mother.

Arto   That is what I guessed. It may surprise you to learn that she was also my wife.

A ROCKY VALLEY

(Tom, Stardust, Annie and Arto are heading back through the rocky valley to the Star-Chaser.*)*

Stardust If this is true, you know what it means, Tom?

Annie It means that his name is Tom Arto.

Tom Thank you, Annie, I had worked that out. Professor, what proof have you got?

Arto I have the same photograph. I carry it with me all the time. I was on a long space journey when your mother died. I knew she was going to have a child, but I thought it had died as well. I was up to no good even then, and no one wanted me to be in charge of a baby,

so they didn't tell me it had lived. When I first saw you, you reminded me of what I was like when I was young. When I saw the photograph in the spaceship, I knew you must be my son, so I decided I didn't want to work for Princess Io any more.

Stardust Come on, we'd better hurry back to the *Star-Chaser*. Your oxygen is getting low, Professor. If we don't hurry, Tom really will be an orphan.

Annie   Are you sure there is no way into the base from the outside, Professor?

Arto   I am certain. I designed the door myself. Once it is locked from the inside, nothing can get in.

Annie   We will have to call the space police after all.

Arto   I don't think even they will break down that door. In any case, Princess Io has other bases. Even I don't know all of them.

Stardust We're nearly back at the ship. We will be there in about ten minutes. You ought just to make it, Professor, but it's going to be close!

Annie   I have bad news, Captain. I can see the *Star-Chaser* – and there is another ship next to it!

Tom   What ship?

Annie   The *Queen of the Night*! Princess Io has tricked us!

OUTSIDE THE
STAR-CHASER

Stardust Io, let us into our ship! You know our oxygen is running out!

Io What a terrible shame! I see you have that traitor Arto with you. Well, I'm really looking forward to watching you all die out there. No, it's no good looking at the *Queen of the Night*. You won't get in there either. The professor is really good at doors you can't open! Open the door? Not a chance! … Hey, Hench, what are you doing?

Hench Opening the door, Princess.

Io Who told you to do that, you stupid machine?

Hench	You did, just now.
Io	No I didn't.
Hench	I wish you would make up your mind!
Stardust	It looks like we're finished. Any ideas, team? Hey, Annie, what are you doing?

(*Annie starts to stagger about, then collapses on the ground.*)

Annie   Help, help! I've run out of oxygen! Please help me, I'm dying!

Hench   Don't worry, Annie. I'll save you!

Tom   Quick, he's opening the air-lock door! Inside, everyone, quick!

Io	You fool! You've fallen for a trick, you useless contraption!
Hench	I couldn't let Annie die! She is such a beautiful android!
Io	She wasn't dying! androids don't need oxygen, you idiot!
Hench	Oh yes, I'd forgotten that. I'll shut the door then.
Stardust	That's a good idea, Hench – we're all inside now.
Io	Stay away from me, Stardust. I have a deadly weapon! Hey, what's happening? I can't move!
Arto	I thought this thread gun from the Rainbow Planet might come in useful. That's why I stole one when we were escaping from the prison cave. Now I'd better deal with Hench before he realises what's going on.
Hench	Professor – what's going on?

Arto   A big change, Hench. We're working for Captain Stardust now.

Hench   That's good. Now I can really be Annie's friend!

Annie   What? Is that robot going to be around all the time from now on? I don't believe it! It can't be true …

Tom   Stop getting so excited, Annie. You said it yourself – it's bad for your microchips!